W9-AGE-801

C++ for Kids™

A fun and visual introduction to the fundamental programing language

by Blaise Vanden-Heuvel & John C. Vanden-Heuvel Sr.

Illustrations by Tom Holmes

KidsFirst.cpp ✕

```cpp
1    //Kid's first C++ program
2    #include <iostream>
3    using namespace std;
4
5    void main ()
6    {
7        cout<<"Hello Little Coder!";
8    }
```

KidsFirst.exe

Output

Hello Little Coder!

Words in **green** are pretend.

The rest are our friends.

Words in **blue** are special.

Words in **red** are said.

```cpp
//3 output statements
#include <iostream>
using namespace std;

void main ()
{
    cout<<"Hello Little Coder!"<<endl;
    cout<<"I love you.\n";
    cout<<"Goodbye.";
}
```

Output

Hello Little Coder!
I love you.
Goodbye.

More words in **red** means more words are said.

More words in **green** are still never seen.

To create new lines use **<<endl.**

You can use '\n' as well.

Airplane.cpp   ✕

```cpp
1    //Airplane output program
2    #include <iostream>
3    using namespace std;
4
5    void main ()
6    {
7        cout<<"     |\ _____ "<<endl;
8        cout<<"   -=\c`'''''''''''   ` ) "<<endl;
9        cout<<"      `~~~~~/  /~~`   "<<endl;
10       cout<<"          -==/  / "<<endl;
11       cout<<"           `-' "<<endl;
12       cout<<endl;
13       cout<<"          _ . "<<endl;
14       cout<<"        ( _ )_"<<endl;
15       cout<<"       (_ _(_ ,) "<<endl;
16   }
```

Output

```
          |\ _____
  -=\c`'''''''''''  `  )
      `~~~~~/   /~~`
       -==/   /
         `_ /

        _ .
      ( ˉ_ )_
     (_  _(_ ,)
```

main() is the best, it is in charge of all the rest.

Without main() there would be no plane.

<<endl ends a line, every time.

Add.cpp

```cpp
1    //How to add in C++
2    #include <iostream>
3    using namespace std;
4
5    void main ()
6    {
7        int a;
8        int b;
9        int c;
10
11       a= 1;
12       b= 2;
13       c= a + b;
14
15       cout<<c;
16   }
```

Output

3

Numbers are also said,

but they aren't in **red**.

cout<<c means the computer says 3.

Array.cpp　✕

```cpp
1    //Learning Arrays
2    #include <iostream>
3    using namespace std;
4
5    void main ()
6    {
7        int a;
8        int b[5];
9
10       a=1;
11
12       b[0]=1;
13       b[1]=2;
14       b[2]=3;
15       b[3]=4;
16       b[4]=5;
17
18       cout<<"Variable a is "<<a<<endl;
19       cout<<"Variable b[4] is "<<b[4];
20   }
```

Output

Variable a is 1

Array b[4] is 5

Variables like 'a' hold only one thing.

That one thing could be a number, a letter or a string.

Arrays like b[ ] can hold a lot. b[ ] has 5 slots.

```cpp
//What is a string?
#include <iostream>
#include <string>
using namespace std;

void main ()
{
    string bird;
    bird="Polly";

    cout<<bird<<"wants a cracker?";
}
```

Output

Polly wants a cracker?

Think of string
as a long rope
that can hold anything.

string **bird** can hold letters,
numbers and words.

Input.cpp

```cpp
1    //Using cin for the first time
2    #include <iostream>
3    using namespace std;
4
5    void main ()
6    {
7        string name;
8        cout<<"Let's play a game,\n";
9        cout<<"type in your name:\n";
10       cin>>name;
11
12   }
```

Hello! My name is...

Output

Let's play a game,
type in your name:

The computer talks with **cout<<**
and listens with **cin>>**

When you see **cin>>**
that is when you type your name in

Say your name
to finish the game!

TrainFunction.cpp ✕

```cpp
1    //Kid's first function
2    #include <iostream>
3    using namespace std;
4    void train ();
5
6    void main ()
7    {
8        train();
9    }
10
11       void train()
12   {
13        cout<<"    _____"<<endl;
14        cout<<"   | _ |      __"<<endl;
15        cout<<"   | | | |_____V_"<<endl;
16        cout<<"   | |_| |       \ "<<endl;
17        cout<<"   |_  |  _  _   |"<<endl;
18        cout<<"   |/ \_|_/ \/ \/ "<<endl;
19        cout<<"    \/    \_/\_/ "<<endl;
20   }
```

Output

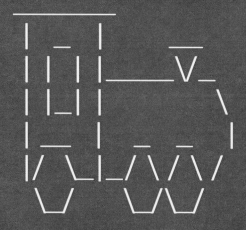

main() is a function and so is train()

train() is inside main()

train() uses main() as a junction
That is how we call a function.

If.cpp ✕

```cpp
1    //How to use an if statement
2    #include <iostream>
3    using namespace std;
4
5    void main ()
6    {
7        if ( 1 >2 )
8            cout<<"1 is larger than 2"<<endl;
9        if ( 2 >1 )
10           cout<<"2 is larger than 1"<<endl;
11   }
```

If.exe

Output

2 is larger than 1

if is always followed by a condition.

if is also in blue.

The computer will then make a decision.

One is not larger than two.

WhileLoop.cpp

```cpp
1   //Using a while loop to repeat
2   #include <iostream>
3   using namespace std;
4
5   void main ()
6   {
7       int age=1;
8       while (age < 5)
9       {
10          cout<<"Jack is "<<age<<" years old.";
11          cout<<"Jack doesn't go to school."<<endl;
12          age++; //age= age+1;
13      }
14   cout<<"Jack is now "<<age<<" years old and can
15          go to school!";
16  }
```

29

Output

Jack is 1 years old. Jack doesn't go to school.

Jack is 2 years old. Jack doesn't go to school.

Jack is 3 years old. Jack doesn't go to school.

Jack is 4 years old. Jack doesn't go to school.

Jack is now 5 years old and can go to school!

while also has a condition and is a **loop**, everything in { } is in its group.

When the condition is true, everything in the group gets a redo.

When the condition is false, the group falls through.

```cpp
1    //Using a for loop to repeat
2    #include <iostream>
3    using namespace std;
4
5    void main ()
6    {
7        //for loop j
8        for (int j = 1; j <6; j++)
9        {
10            cout<<"*";
11        }
12        cout<<endl<<endl;
13
14        //for loop k
15        for (int k=1; k<6; k++)
16        {
17            cout<<"*"<<endl;
18        }
19    }
```

Output

```
******

   *
   *
   *
   *
   *
   *
```

for is another type of **loop**,
it goes around like a hula-hoop.

Both loops go from **1** to **6**,
every time outputting an asterisk.

The only difference between **loop j** and **k**
is that they go in a different way.

Glossary

compiler
A computer program that translates C++ language
into machine language so the computer can understand it.

#include
Tells the compiler to refer to another, already created file.
Use <> to surround the file name.

iostream
Said as [I O stream] for Input and Output. A previously
created file that adds the use of input and output.

using namespace std
Said as [using namepace standard]. A commonly used
statement that includes std:: before standards like cout
and cin so we don't have to

cout
Said as [c out]. The standard output
for the language.

cin

Said as [c in]. The standard input for the language.

<<

Insertion Operator. Used with cout to display text or values.

>>

Extraction Operator. Used with cin to obtain values or other input from the user.

//

Designates any preceding information as comments and are ignored by the compiler.

;

Ends a c/c++ statement. Very similar to the way a period (.) ends a sentence in the English language.

" "

Used with cout to output text within the quotations.

void

Data/return type that allows a null (empty or invalid) value.

int

Data/return type that allows identifiers to store an integer.

string

Data/return type that allows identifiers to store a group of characters. Since string is not included in the iostream file, to use it, #include<string>.

main ()

Necessary and primary function that executes code.

function

A group of statements that are executed when the function name is called in main.

array

Allows identifiers to store multiple data.
The number within the braces is how many
pieces of data it can store. int **A[2]** is said
[**array A sub 2**]. Array A can hold 2 integers.

identifier

The name of a variable, which is made known to the
compiler by using data types.

if

A statement that lets the computer make
a choice based on the condition.

for/while Loop

A statement that repeats until the condition
proves false.

endl \n

Used to visually end a line when using cout.

We would love to hear from you!
Say hi :-) at:

codebabies.com
Facebook.com/CodeBabiesBooks
Twitter: @codebabies

Made in United States
North Haven, CT
09 June 2022

20048606R00018